ANCIENT EARTH JOURNAL

THE LATE JURASSIC:

VOLUME 2

NOTES, DRAWINGS, AND OBSERVATIONS FROM PREHISTORY

BY JUAN CARLOS ALONSO & GREGORY S. PAUL

Walter Foster
Jr.

For Betty and Dalí, your undying support and endless inspiration make everything worthwhile.
Love, Juan Carlos.

This library edition published in 2017 by Walter Foster Jr.,
an imprint of The Quarto Group
6 Orchard Road, Suite 100
Lake Forest, CA 92630

Distributed in the United States and Canada by
Lerner Publisher Services
241 First Avenue North
Minneapolis, MN 55401 U.S.A.
www.lernerbooks.com

First Library Edition

Library of Congress Cataloging-in-Publication Data

Names: Alonso, Juan Carlos (Graphic designer), author, illustrator. | Paul, Gregory S., author.
Title: The late Jurassic : notes, drawings, and observations from prehistory
    / by Juan Carlos Alonso & Gregory S. Paul.
Other titles: Ancient Earth journal.
Description: First library edition. | Lake Forest, CA : Walter Foster Jr., an
    imprint of Quarto Publishing Group USA Inc., 2017. | Series: Ancient Earth
    journal | Audience: Ages 8+. | Includes bibliographical references and index.
Identifiers: LCCN 2017011686 | ISBN 9781942875321 (volume 1 : hardcover : alk.
    paper) | ISBN 9781942875338 (volume 2 : hardcover : alk. paper)
Subjects: LCSH: Paleontology--Jurassic--Juvenile literature. |
    Dinosaurs--Juvenile literature. | Animals, Fossil--Juvenile literature. |
    CYAC: Prehistoric animals.
Classification: LCC QE733 .A46 2017 | DDC 560.1766--dc23
LC record available at https://lccn.loc.gov/2017011686

Printed in USA
9 8 7 6 5 4 3 2 1

Table of Contents

Foreword

Matthew T. Mossbrucker

Director & Chief Curator

Morrison Natural History Museum, Morrison, Colorado

Jurassic! For kids (and some adults), this word immediately brings to mind images of giant dinosaurs crashing and smashing their way through a dim, primeval forest while a volcano explodes somewhere in the distance. When I was a kid reading dinosaur books like this one, I was surprised to learn that the Jurassic wasn't a where like that imaginary forest, but a when.

The word "Jurassic" refers to a special time in the history of our planet, beginning 201 million years ago and ending about 145 million years ago. Our planet is old—really, really old. The Earth is so old that we use words to tell time instead of clocks. Giving names to periods from Earth's history helps us chart time, similar to how a calendar helps us talk about when events happened in the past. "When were you born?" my kids ask me, and I say "May of 1979." When we talk about dinosaurs, they ask "When did Stegosaurus live?" and I say "The Jurassic."

The Jurassic lasted for so long that it is broken up into smaller pieces, kind of like a year is broken down into months. The Jurassic is first divided into three big chunks of time called "Early," "Middle," and "Late." Then it is divided again into even smaller time-chunks with formal names like "Oxfordian," as well as ten others. Fifty-six million years is a long time, and no dinosaur lived for the entire Jurassic period.

Fossils are the remains of living things preserved in stone that was once mud or sand. Dinosaur fossils are only found in specific layers of rock that were deposited as sand and dirt during a small part of the Jurassic. These remains help us learn about what lived during the Jurassic.

Some of the most famous dinosaurs lived during the Late Jurassic. Fossils of the spike-tailed Stegosaurus and the fearsome birdlike Allosaurus are found together in western North America, along with the giant dino-cousins, Apatosaurus and Brontosaurus. Not all dinosaurs lived at the same time or even in the same place. The oldest dinosaurs of the Early Jurassic are remarkable, like the ancestor of Stegosaurus, the armor-studded Scelidosaurus from England.

The first Jurassic dinosaur fossils found were named Megalosaurus in 1824. They were from Middle Jurassic age rocks in England. Megalosaurus fossils helped define what it means to be a dinosaur. Middle Jurassic fossils remain elusive to this day. In fact, modern paleontologists are still discovering new animals and plants from extinct streams and ponds that once offered Jurassic dinosaurs a drink.

As you read this book, think about each dinosaur and what its life might have been like. Take a trip to your library and read as many dinosaur books as you can find. Visit your local museum and learn more about the dinosaurs that might have lived in your own backyard.

Introduction

Come along with us on a journey deep into the earth's history, to a time long before the first humans ever existed. A time when giants roamed the earth and reptiles ruled the skies. A time of absolute beauty and extreme danger—this is the Late Jurassic.

We are now about 150 million years away from the earth as we know it. Standing in lush green surroundings, you take a deep breath and notice how thick the air is with humidity. The unique smell of wet and decomposing plant matter overwhelms you as the sound of insects rings endlessly in your ears. The air is stifling hot, making it exhausting to get around. The Late Jurassic does not welcome visitors.

MESOZOIC ERA

245 Million Years Ago   208 Million Years Ago   162 Million Years Ago   145 Million Years Ago   65 Million Years Ago

Permian   TRIASSIC PERIOD   JURASSIC PERIOD   CRETACEOUS PERIOD

LATE JURASSIC

The Jurassic period is the middle portion of the Mesozoic era, better known as "the age of reptiles." During the latter part of this period, the earth is experiencing significant changes, including volcanic activity due to shifting tectonic plates. The once supercontinent, Pangaea, is now divided into four landmasses consisting of South America and Africa, Western Europe and Asia, Australia and Antarctica, and North America.

The eruptions from volcanoes along with greenhouse gasses are raising temperatures worldwide, several degrees warmer than in modern times. Because of this, there are no polar ice caps, leading to extremely high sea levels. The two largest bodies of water, the Pacific Ocean and the Tethys Ocean, take up 80 percent of the earth's surface, while the Atlantic Ocean is just beginning to appear as a small inland sea. The world is a warm, wet, and tropical place—the perfect environment for plant and animal development.

The earth during the Late Jurassic

Around you the landscape is composed of tall conifer trees like the Araucaria (see fig. a) and Ginkgo trees. Low lying club mosses (see fig. b) and Neocalamites, or horsetail plants (see fig. c), stem from and around freshwater ponds and creeks. Ferns and cycads, like Otozamites (see fig. d), dominate as ground cover and low trees. Everywhere you look you are surrounded by greenery. This greenery fuels the growth of enormous plant-eating dinosaurs.

Some dinosaur species are rapidly evolving larger in a race to outgrow the predators that feed on them, some reaching lengths of over 100 feet. As groups of dinosaurs, such as the sauropods, evolve into larger species, so do their predators. Animals like Allosaurus and Torvosaurus are becoming apex predators reaching over 30 feet in length, armed with weaponry designed to dispatch their prey quickly and efficiently. While some herbivorous dinosaurs are finding safety in size, others are beginning to develop armor or speed as a way to elude the jaws of predators.

Mature tree can grow in excess of 100 ft. tall

Root system extends for several yards, giving the plant a large area of coverage

Seed cone detail

Leaf detail

Soil level

Figure a. Araucaria Tree

Figure b. Club Moss

Danger comes in all sizes, as smaller predators are filling evolutionary niches and becoming specialized hunters. Gliding through the air from trees is becoming a new means of hunting for the smaller theropod dinosaurs. This method will soon give rise to the first true birds. But for now, pterosaurs, or "flying reptiles," are the undisputed rulers of the sky. Though diminutive in size, their adaptations and ability for flight are unmatched by any other vertebrates.

Continue along on our journey as we dive deeper into the wildlife of the Late Jurassic than ever before, coming face to face with everything from early mammals to super predators. In this book, you will discover how some dinosaurs developed techniques for hunting while others used new adaptations for self-defense. Page by page, you'll see a first-hand, intimate account of what it was like to stand ankle-high next to the largest group of animals to walk the earth. These animals towered over our closest relatives—the early mammals—as they began to stake their claim in a world dominated by dinosaurs. This is the Late Jurassic as never seen before.

Neocalamites live beneath the level of soil, allowing them to regenerate quickly after being consumed by animals

Soil level

Mature plant

Figure c. Neocalamites

Mature plant

Leaf detail

Figure d. Otozamites

The Sauropods

Our journey continues deep into the Late Jurassic to explore the largest land animals ever: the sauropods. Spread before you are vast forests of early pine trees reaching as high as 100 feet above the ground. At your feet are beds of thick green ferns and cycad plants covering the ground like an endless carpet, with intermittent dark tree trunks breaking up the green color. Pterosaurs glide through the air, effortlessly picking up insects without ever breaking their rhythm. It is generally silent with the occasional squawk of a pterosaur and the snap of branches from the trees above. As you look up, a thick neck extends upward, ending in an almost imperceptible head. It forcefully pulls back, breaking another branch. At the base of the neck is a colossal body held up by four pillar-like legs. This animal is so big, it cannot be seen all at once.

It quietly goes about its business as another much heavier and longer animal joins in, turning its attention to the lower plants. It strips the leaves from entire fern plants systematically with its mouth, one at a time, moving its neck from plant to plant while keeping its body still.

Others begin to appear through the trees, each oblivious to one another as they continue to feed. You are in the unmistakable company of sauropods.

Sauropods were by far the heaviest and longest land animals to ever exist. They were known for their large, elephant-like bodies with long necks and tails. Though most were gigantic, some species only reached the size of a large bull.

Regardless of their size, all were designed to be efficient eaters. Some consumed hundreds of pounds of plant matter daily in order to maintain their mass. Sauropod heads were typically small with teeth lining the front edges of their jaws. They did not chew or crush plants with their mouths, but rather swallowed them whole. Their teeth were specialized for two different eating techniques: stripping or tearing. Peg-like teeth (fig. a) were for stripping the leaves from a plant; chiseled teeth (fig. b) were for tearing and cutting leaves and branches. Teeth were shed and replaced as needed every few days to every few months as they wore down.

Sauropods' large, bloated trunks contained fermentation chambers called "caecum," which processed raw plant matter and extracted nutrients

Top view

Figure a

Diplodocus tooth

Side view

Front view   Side view

Top view

Figure b

Camarasaurus tooth

starting at the gizzard and continuing all the way through the intestines. Their necks were also instrumental in eating. Most species evolved long necks for either reaching higher-growing plants or covering a large area of low-lying plants without having to move their bodies.

To counterbalance their heavy necks and torsos, sauropods evolved heavy tails. These tails became specialized as well, some becoming defensive weapons with long whips or hammer-like clubs.

Sauropods hatched from eggs and were born precocial, meaning they were fully capable of feeding and walking without assistance from their parents. Nests were usually communal, consisting of many individuals laying eggs in one area. Like modern sea turtles, only a small percentage of sauropod hatchlings survived predation and made it into adulthood. Of the surviving few, juveniles formed groups and eventually herds, seeking safety in numbers.

Sauropods of the Late Jurassic

The Late Jurassic is known as "the era of giants." Sauropods evolved and flourished into species more gigantic than the earth has ever or will ever see again. It is during this period that some of the most recognizable dinosaurs, like the Brontosaurus and Diplodocus, live. The Late Jurassic landscape was abundant with herds of great sauropods moving in a constant search for food.

This section explores three basic families of sauropods. First the Diplodocidae, known for their long horizontal bodies, teeth at the front of their mouths, and long whipping tails which made up about half of their overall body length. This group includes species like Brontosaurus louisae and Diplodocus hallorum. Second, the Camarasauridae family, with relatively short upright necks and larger heads, with the nasal opening in their skull ahead of their eyes. This family is represented by its namesake Camarasaurus supremus. And finally, the Brachiosauridae family, best known for their giraffe-like posture, with their forelimbs longer than their hind limbs, causing them to carry their necks vertically. This family is represented by one of the best-studied species: Giraffatitan brancai.

In the following pages, explore these magnificent animals in detail and see their specialized adaptations for both eating and survival.

A newborn Brachiosaurus hatchling makes its way out of its egg and joins others seeking safety

Long, rectangular head

Long, thick, and deep neck

Tall ridge along back

Small eyes

Short forelimbs

Long jaw

Narrow, blunt teeth for stripping leaves off plants

Brontosaurus louisae

Location Observed: *Utah, United States*

Family: *Diplodocidae*

Length: *75 feet (23 meters)*

Height: *17 feet (5.2 meters)*

Weight: *20 tons*

Temperament: *Defensive, aggressive*

Long tail with whip-like end

Tall, robust hind limbs

9 feet
6 feet
3 feet

For many years, Brontosaurus louisae went by the name Apatosaurus louisae

Almost impossible to attack from behind— Brontosaurus' tail acts like a whip, capable of inflicting harm to any attacker that comes from behind

The tip of its tail is capable of reaching speeds faster than sound, creating a loud snapping sound like a whip

Legs and feet are directly underneath the body

Tall neural spines act like a suspension bridge supporting the neck and tail

Massively built neck

Forefeet are considerably smaller than hind feet and only contain one toenail

Brontosaurus leaves large prints in the dry mud. These impressions show how its gait was similar to that of a modern elephant.

A small theropod drinks water unearthed by the heavy sauropod's footprint

Tail is more than 50 percent of Brontosaurus' total length

Large, four-toed hind feet

Short, blunt head

Large head for
a sauropod

Relatively thick,
short neck

Hind right foot
of Camarasaurus
is broad and designed
to carry the full
weight of the animal

Front right foot
is much smaller
and built much
lighter than the
hind feet

Tall shoulders

Forelimbs shorter
than hind limbs

Single-toed forefeet

Camarasaurus supremus

Location Observed: Colorado, Wyoming, and Utah, United States

Family: Camarasauridae

Length: 50 feet (15 meters)

Height: 17 feet (5.2 meters)

Weight: 15 tons

Temperament: Social, cautious

Small eyes

Dome on top of head

Long, narrow tail

Large, chiseled teeth designed for cutting leaves and branches

Four-toed hind feet

9 feet

6 feet

3 feet

Compared to most of the giant sauropods of the Late Jurassic, Camarasaurus supremus is considered medium-sized

9 feet

6 feet

3 feet

Diplodocus is extremely long, but built lighter than most of the other giant sauropods

High ridge along back
and base of tail

Dermal spines
running from
head to tail

Very long tail ending
in a whip-like tip

Powerfully built
hind limbs

Thinner, shorter
forelimbs

Diplodocus hallorum

Location Observed: *Colorado and Utah, United States*

Family: *Diplodocidae*

Length: *80 feet (25 meters)*

Height: *20 feet (6 meters)*

Weight: *12 tons*

Temperament: *Social, cautious*

Flat and wide mouth

Long, narrow neck

Large nostrils

Forward facing, peg-like teeth

Long, rectangular head

Using its 40-foot-long muscular tail as a defensive weapon, Diplodocus whips back and forth preventing any attacker from getting close

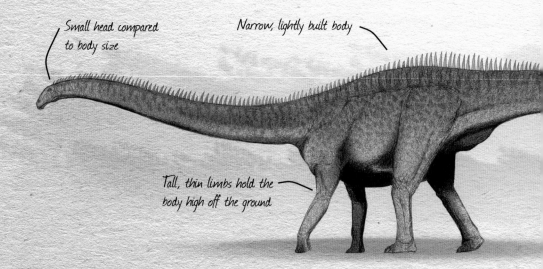

Small head compared to body size

Narrow, lightly built body

Tall, thin limbs hold the body high off the ground

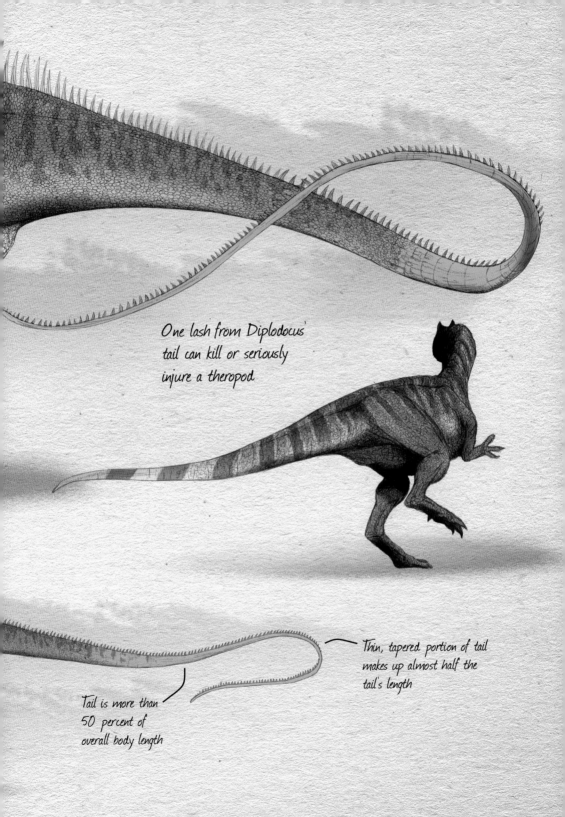

One lash from Diplodocus'
tail can kill or seriously
injure a theropod

Thin, tapered portion of tail
makes up almost half the
tail's length

Tail is more than
50 percent of
overall body length

Giraffatitan brancai

Location Observed: *Tanzania, Africa*

Family: *Brachiosauridae*

Length: *75 feet (23 meters)*

Height: *50 feet (15 meters)*

Weight: *40 tons*

Temperament: *Defensive, aggressive*

9 feet
6 feet
3 feet

For many years, Giraffatitan brancai was known as Brachiosaurus brancai

Back slopes upward

Tail much shorter than neck

Short hind limbs

Small head

Long, thick neck

Deep, short head

Large dome on top of head

Large nostrils

Deep shoulders

Long forelimbs

Rounded mouth with evenly spaced-out teeth

Peg-like teeth for stripping leaves off trees

The Ornithischians

It's a foggy morning as the Jurassic sun begins to rise over a field of horsetail plants. As you walk into a field, trees slowly begin to appear through the fog, making themselves more visible with each step you take. There is a drone of insects and mosquitoes in your ear, punctuated by the low grunts and snorting sounds coming from a nearby large animal. The air is thick with humidity and the odor of dung, reminiscent of a farm or petting zoo. The grunting noises continue just ahead of you, as a towering object begins to take shape through the fog. The object moves away from you as it slowly reveals itself—it's an immense dinosaur feeding on the plants beneath it. A cloud of insects forms around its nose and lands on its nostrils. With another deep snort from the dinosaur, the insects disband before reassembling. Its head moves downward as it takes in a mouthful of horsetail plants. Using its hardened beak, it cuts the plants cleanly, then crushes them with its teeth and swallows.

6 feet

3 feet

It is now in plain sight. The unmistakable plates on its back tell you it's a Stegosaurus and it's massive—over 12 feet tall and 20 feet long, about the size of a modern-day elephant. As you approach to get a closer look, the Stegosaurus becomes agitated and begins to rear up as if to say "stay away." This behavior is no different than approaching any wild animal that feels threatened. The fog has now almost entirely lifted, and more animals in the field are now visible. You realize that you are standing among dozens of dinosaurs, all grazing on the same pasture of plants. Many species of ornithischian dinosaurs have come together to peacefully feed, as they have many times in the past. This is a typical breakfast in the Late Jurassic.

Camptosaurus dispar skeleton

Ornithischians were one of the two major orders of dinosaurs, the other being saurichian (which includes theropods and sauropods). They were known for their hip structure, beaked mouths, and for being herbivores or "plant eaters." Ornithischians were an extremely diverse group, including many different body types and self-defense methods. Even their means of locomotion was diverse: some were bipedal (walking on two legs), others were quadrupedal (walking on four legs), while many were capable of switching between both. If you compare ornithischians to modern-day animals, they would be considered large prey animals, such as horses, cattle, rhinoceroses, and even elephants, as they all had very different body types and means of self-defense, and yet were all herbivorous. Some of the more famous ornithischian dinosaurs include Stegosaurus, Triceratops (Late Cretaceous), Ankylosaurus (Cretaceous), and Hadrosaurs or "duck-billed dinosaurs" (Late Cretaceous).

Ornithischians of the Late Jurassic

By the Late Jurassic, most ornithischians had clearly developed means by which to confront or escape predators—none more evident than the Stegosaurus stenops and Kentrosaurus aethiopicus. Both dinosaurs had tails clad with sharp, spiked horns and plates rising from their backs. With this deterrent, few, if any, predators were willing to challenge a healthy adult. Kentrosaurus even had 3-foot-long spikes protruding from its shoulders to avoid ambush from the sides. Others like Gargoyleosaurus parkpinorum preferred a passive form of self-defense. Built wide, low to the ground, and armored literally from the nose to the tip of its tail, Gargoyleosaurus made itself a difficult meal to be had. This dinosaur was the ancestor of future dinosaurs from the Cretaceous, like Ankylosaurus, which developed more active forms of self-defense by using a bony growth on the tip of its tail as a club to ward off attackers. Other species like Camptosaurus dispar evolved with larger hind limbs and smaller forelimbs. Because of this, it could outrun many of its predators. When given no means of escape, Camptosaurus was also equipped with a large thumb claw used as a formidable weapon.

Explore the ornithischian dinosaurs in the following pages, and see how they survived the dangers of the Late Jurassic.

Camptosaurus dispar

Location Observed: Wyoming, United States

Family: Camptosauridae

Length: 16 feet (5 meters)

Height: 6 feet (1.8 meters)

Weight: 1,000 pounds

Temperament: Reclusive, shy

Relatively long neck

Tall back

Small head

Short forelimbs

Five fingers on hand,
including a thumb spike

Brow shading above eyes give Camptosaurus an angry look

Very large eyes

Cheeks conceal grinding teeth

Beak designed for cutting plant matter

Camptosaurus hatchling

Large thumb spike

Fifth digit is underdeveloped

Camptosaurus left hand detail

Wide, long tail

Robust, powerful hind legs

6 feet

3 feet

The name Camptosaurus means "bent lizard." It was given this name because of its hunched stance.

Gargoyleosaurus parkpinorum

Location Observed: Wyoming, United States

Family: Nodosauridae

Length: 9 feet (3 meters)

Height: 3 feet (1 meter)

Weight: 600 pounds

Temperament: Defensive, aggressive

Its hardened, dome-shaped carapace is impenetrable

Tail ends in a bare tip

Powerful tail lined with spikes

Fused scales creating armor above hips

Short stocky limbs

6 feet

3 feet

Gargoyleosaurus is short, but it can defend itself from large predators.

Fused scales to top
of head

Horns above and below eyes

Small teeth

Triangular-shaped head

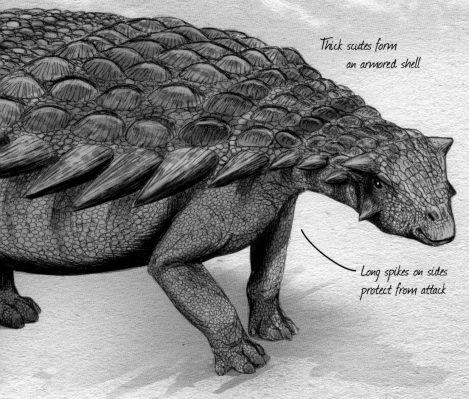

Thick scutes form
an armored shell

Long spikes on sides
protect from attack

Long, rectangular head

Beak designed for cutting low-lying plants

Grinding teeth behind cheeks

Seven rows of flat plates along neck and back

Small head

Relatively long neck

Short forelimbs

Enormous spikes protruding from shoulders

Kentrosaurus aethiopicus

Location Observed: *Tanzania, Africa*

Family: *Stegosauridae*

Length: *13 feet (4 meters)*

Height: *5 feet (1.5 meters)*

Weight: *1,500 pounds*

Temperament: *Defensive, aggressive*

Seven rows of long spikes from mid-back to end of tail

Long, thick tail

Large hind limbs

6 feet

3 feet

Kentrosaurus is much smaller than its American cousin, Stegosaurus

Stegosaurus stenops

Location Observed: Colorado, United States

Family: Stegosauridae

Length: 21 feet (6.5 meters)

Height: 12 feet (3.5 meters)

Weight: 3.5 tons

Temperament: Aggressive

Alternating row of
17 armor plates used
mostly as display

Short, deep, and
narrow torso

Small head with short neck

Five-toed forefeet

Long, narrow head

Small teeth line
the sides of jaws

Thick, bony scales serve
as protective armor
around neck

Four tail spikes used
for defense

Muscular and deep tail

Hind limbs twice the
length of its forelimbs

9 feet

6 feet

3 feet

Three-toed hind feet

Stegosaurus is a large and extremely dangerous dinosaur

A healthy, adult Stegosaurus has few enemies. Its size, weight, and spiked tail make any predator think twice.

Rearing up on two legs makes Stegosaurus appear larger when threatened

Four long tail spikes at
the end of a powerful and
flexible tail can easily kill
any predator

Stegosaurus tail detail

Hatchling and juvenile
Stegosaurus find security and
protection from predators by
staying close to adults

At a couple years old, this
juvenile Stegosaurus reaches
5 feet in length and already
has tail spikes

The Pterosaurs

It's late afternoon, almost dusk, as the sun begins to approach the Jurassic horizon. The evening will be a welcome relief as the sun takes its relentless heat with it as it sets. The day's end signals the arrival of new animals, as well as a new look to the landscape. The last rays of the sun's light accent the millions of insects dotting the air, almost like a cloud. There are mayflies, mosquitoes, damselflies, and dragonflies all moving at different speeds, slowly stirring the cloud they form. With long slashes, larger flying animals begin to cut through the air like a knife. There are dozens of them all feeding on the assortment of insects floating before them. They consist of two body types: one is larger with a pointed beak and tail ending in a diamond-shaped rudder; the other is much smaller with a rounded head.

With effortless precision, they pierce the air and snap up their prey, zigzagging and narrowly missing one another as if they've rehearsed this intricate dance. The largest of them has a wingspan about the size of an eagle, while the smallest species is no bigger than a blue jay. One swoops inches from your head as you feel the wind rush past you and hear the quick flapping of its wings. You are an eyewitness to the daily feast of the pterosaurs: the absolute masters of flight during the Late Jurassic.

Pterosaurs, which means "winged reptile" in ancient Greek, were the first vertebrates to evolve self-sufficient flight millions of years before mammals (bats) or even birds.

They flew using the same principles modern birds use today, with wings made from a fibrous membrane extending from their elongated fourth fingers and attached to their hind limbs. Pterosaurs' anatomy was designed to be very efficient for flight. Its skeleton included a system of air sacs that worked with the lungs to aid in respiration and reduce body weight. Pterosaur skeletons were constructed of a strong framework of hollow bones, with skulls containing openings called "fenestra" to help reduce weight without sacrificing structural support. They were truly a masterpiece of engineering.

Pterosaurs of the Late Jurassic

By the Late Jurassic, pterosaurs had evolved specialized adaptations for hunting and flight. Species like Rhamphorhynchus muensteri were equipped with thin, forward-facing teeth designed to spear insects and fish in mid-flight. Its curved beak also had sharpened tips on both the skull and jaw to ensure prey didn't escape. Rhamphorhynchus was also known for its long, rigid tail, which it used as a counterbalance, much like the tail of a kite. By swinging its tail, it could change direction and control its flight at will. Anurognathus ammoni, by comparison, flew without the aid of a long tail for balance. Its long, slender wings and rounded frog-like face were more suited for flying in tighter quarters between trees and obstacles where it too hunted for insects in midair. Anurognathus also had large, evolved eyes to allow for vision in low-light conditions, making it an excellent nocturnal hunter.

Fenestra (skull openings)

Fourth finger extends
to form leading edge
of wing

Third finger

Second finger

First finger

Shoulder

Elbow

Small torso,
about the size
of its head

Rhamphorhynchus muensteri skeleton

Thin, light legs

Tail stiffened by tendons

These two species set the wheels of evolution in motion for what
would later become the flying giants of the Cretaceous. In the
following pages, take a closer look at two of the rulers of the Late
Jurassic skies.

Anurognathus ammoni

Location Observed: *Germany*

Family: *Anurognathidae*

Length: *6 inches (.15 meter)*

Height: *20 inches (.5 meter) wingspan*

Weight: *5 grams*

Temperament: *Elusive*

Very short, round face

Wide mouth

Large eyes for nocturnal hunting

Three-fingered hands

Head, neck, and torso are covered in thin hair-like fibers

Thin, pin-like teeth designed for catching insects midair

Using its strong muscles, Anurognathus launches itself into the air by leaping forward and pushing off with its forelimbs

6 feet

3 feet

Anurognathus is one of the smallest pterosaurs ever discovered

Short tail

Curved claws on feet

Rhamphorhynchus muensteri

Location Observed: *Germany*

Family: *Rhamphorhynchidae*

Length: *4 feet (1.26 meters)*

Height: *5 feet, 9 inches (1.81 meters) wingspan*

Weight: *2.5 pounds*

Temperament: *Reclusive, shy*

Appendage from wrists acts like an anchor for its wing membrane

Right foot detail

Diamond-shaped rudder at end of tail

Large eyes

Four long and flexible toes with hooked claws

Long, pointed beak

Forward facing, needle-like teeth

Sharp hook at tip of beak

Four toes on each foot

Body covered in fibrous hair

Webbing between toes

Large head

Stiff tail

Three fingers with claws

Membrane from fourth finger, extending to knee, makes up wing

6 feet

3 feet

Rhamphorhynchus is about the size of a hawk

47

Pronunciation Key

Sauropods (Sore-uh-pods)
Brontosaurus louisae (Bron-toe-sore-us, louise-ay)
Camarasaurus supremus (Kam-ara-sore-us, sue-preme-us)
Diplodocus hallorum (Di-plod-oh-kus, hall-ore-um)
Giraffatitan brancai (Ji-raf-a-tie-tan, bran-kai)

Ornithischians (Ore-ni-thisk-key-ahns)
Camptosaurus dispar (Kamp-toe-sore-us, dis-par)
Gargoyleosaurus parkpinorum (Gar-goy-lo-sore-us, park-pin-ore-um)
Kentrosaurus aethiopicus (Ken-tro-sore-us, ethi-opee-cus)
Stegosaurus stenops (Steg-go-sore-us, sten-opps)

Pterosaurs (Ter-uh-sore)
Anurognathus ammoni (An-your-og-nath-us, am-mon-i)
Rhamphorhynchus muensteri (Ram-for-ink-uss, moon-stery)

About the Authors

Juan Carlos Alonso
Juan Carlos Alonso (author and illustrator) is a Cuban American graphic designer, creative director, and illustrator. He has over 30 years experience in the graphic design/illustration field. In 1992 he founded Alonso & Company, a creative boutique specializing in branding, design, and advertising. His passion for nature has taken him around the world, from Australia to the Galapagos Islands, to study animals. Along with his work in the graphic arts, he is also an accomplished wildlife sculptor, focusing mostly on prehistoric animals.

Gregory S. Paul
Gregory S. Paul (co-author) is an American freelance researcher, author, and illustrator who works in paleontology. He is best known for his work and research on theropod dinosaurs and his detailed illustrations, both live and skeletal. Professionally investigating and restoring dinosaurs for three decades, Paul received an on-screen credit as a dinosaur specialist on *Jurassic Park* and Discovery Channel's *When Dinosaurs Roamed America* and *Dinosaur Planet*. He is the author and illustrator of *Predatory Dinosaurs of the World* (1988), *The Complete Illustrated Guide to Dinosaur Skeletons* (1996), *Dinosaurs of the Air* (2001), *The Princeton Field Guide To Dinosaurs* (2010), *Gregory S. Paul's Dinosaur Coffee Table Book* (2010), and editor of *The Scientific American Book of Dinosaurs* (2000). Paul has named over twelve prehistoric animal species and has had two dinosaur species named after him (*Cryptovolans pauli* and *Sellacoxa pauli*) based on his innovative theories.